P9-BTN-095

Girls
are
Girls
and
Boys
are
Boys

Girls are Girls and Boys are Boys

So What's the Difference?

Sol Gordon

Illustrated by
Vivien Cohen

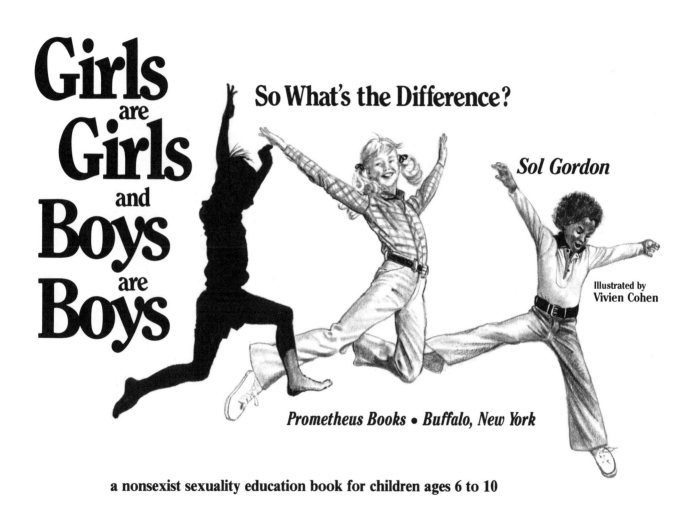

Prometheus Books • Buffalo, New York

a nonsexist sexuality education book for children ages 6 to 10

Published 1991 by Prometheus Books

Revised edition 1985
Text Copyright © 1979 by Sol Gordon
Illustrations Copyright © 1979 by Vivien Cohen

Library of Congress Cataloging-in-Publication Data

Gordon, Sol, 1923–
Girls are girls and boys are boys.

SUMMARY: Briefly explains the facts of human reproduction, the
physical differences between boys and girls, and the fact that these
differences have no effect on a person's choice of career or other interests.
1. Sex education for children. 2. Sex role—Juvenile literature.
(1. Reproduction. 2. Sex role).

HQ53.G6   612.6′007
ISBN 0-87975-686-1

All rights reserved. No part of this publication may be reproduced, stored
in a retrieval system, transmitted in any form or by any means, electronic,
mechanical, photocopying, recording, or otherwise, without prior written
permission of the publisher, except in the case of brief quotations
embodied in critical articles and reviews. Inquiries should be addressed to
Prometheus Books, 700 East Amherst Street, Buffalo, New York 14215,
716–837–2475/FAX 716–835–6901.

Printed in the United States of America on acid-free paper.

CURR
HQ
53
.G6
1991

Do all boys want to become pilots or firemen? Is blue a boy's color? Do all girls want to become mothers or secretaries? Is pink a girl's color?

Baloney!

Lots of boys want to be teachers or to play house. And lots of girls want to be doctors or climb trees. And all of us have our own favorite colors.

Of course, there are differences between girls and boys. Their bodies are different from the moment they are born and become even more so as they grow up.

But a girl can be anything she wants to be, and a boy can be anything he wants to be. Everyone is human—even though girls are girls and boys are boys.

Not too long ago
people used to think
that boys were different
from girls because

boys were supposed
to like climbing trees,

acting rough, and playing ball.

Boys wanted to
become firemen,
airplane pilots,
truck drivers,
or doctors.

And little boys were often dressed in blue clothes by their parents.

**Parents often chose pink
for little girls' clothing.**

Girls were thought to be different from boys because girls liked talking a lot, acting nice, and playing house.

Girls were expected to become mothers, cleaning ladies, or cooks.

And before they got married
they might like working as
secretaries, nurses,
or teachers for a while.

But
all
that
is

A LOT OF BALONEY!

Lots of girls like to climb trees.
Some become doctors,
lawyers, or engineers.

Some don't want to get married
or become mothers.

And almost no one
enjoys cleaning house.

Some boys think playing house is more fun than playing with trucks or airplanes.

**Many boys want to become
teachers, social workers, or nurses.**

But, of course, there are *some* differences between girls and boys.

Girls have a vulva.

Boys have a penis.

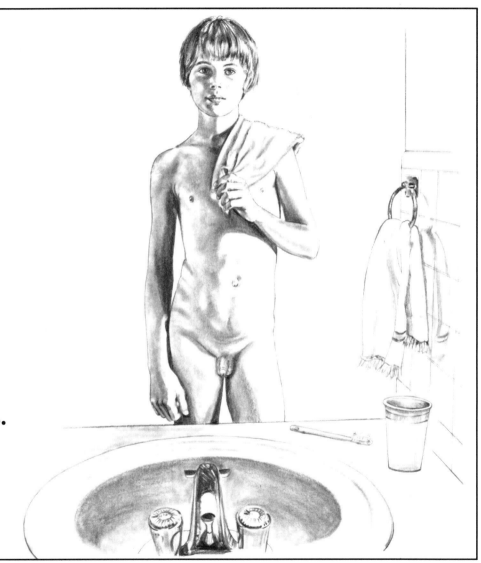

Most boys and girls marry someone they love
when they grow up. If they want to have a child,
the man puts his penis into the woman's vagina.
That's called sexual intercourse.

Most of the time people have sexual
intercourse because it feels good,
and not because they want to have a baby.
So they use birth control, which prevents
a woman from becoming pregnant.

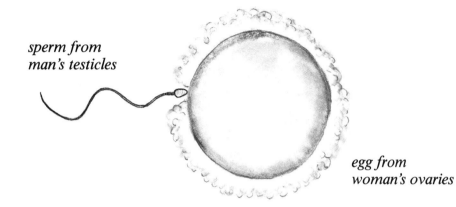

sperm from man's testicles

egg from woman's ovaries

During sexual intercourse if the sperm made in the man's testicles comes out of his penis and unites with an egg from the woman's ovaries, a baby gets started.

The baby grows inside the mother's uterus for 9 months.

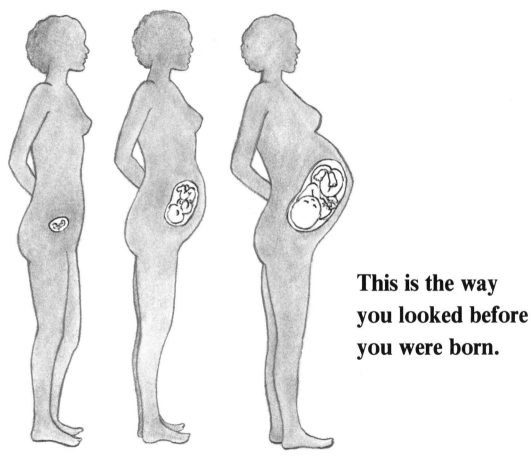

after 2 months   6 months   just before birth

This is the way you looked before you were born.

When you were born you came out through your mother's vagina.

A baby can be fed
with a bottle, or the
mother can breast-feed
her newborn baby.

The most important thing
for the baby is that
it is held,
cuddled,
and loved.

There are a few differences between girls and boys that show up when they are about 12 years old.

A girl's breasts grow larger.

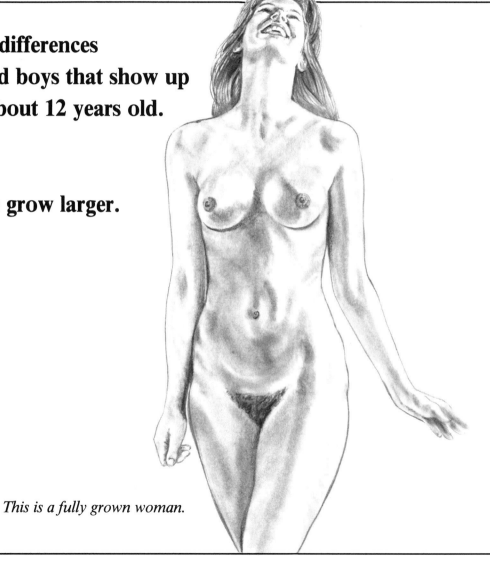

This is a fully grown woman.

Girls also begin to menstruate. Once a month for a few days blood tissue is passed through the vagina.

They put on a pad or use a tampon, which prevents their clothing from getting soiled.

At about 12 years of age a boy
finds that sometimes his penis
becomes big and hard.
At times, semen, which contains
sperm, comes out of his penis
while he is asleep.
This is called a wet dream.*
It also occurs when he fondles
his penis.

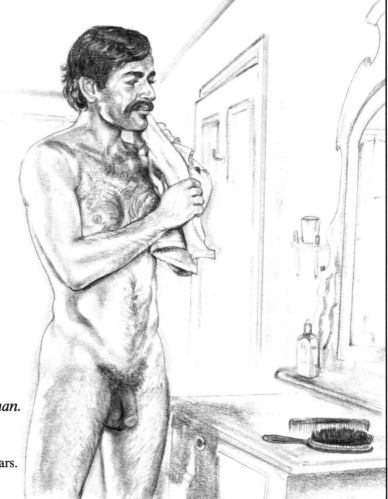

This is a fully grown man.

*This will most likely begin between the ages of 11 and 14 years.

**Masturbation is a big word
for rubbing or stroking
the penis or vagina.
It's an enjoyable feeling
for both boys and girls.**

**Other body changes occur.
Do you know what they are?**

People's feelings change as they grow.

**While they're young, girls
usually make friends with girls.**

Boys usually make friends with boys. But really, it is fun to play with both boys and girls.

For most people things change
when they become teenagers.
Girls keep their girlfriends
and begin enjoying boyfriends.
Boys keep their boyfriends
and begin enjoying girlfriends.

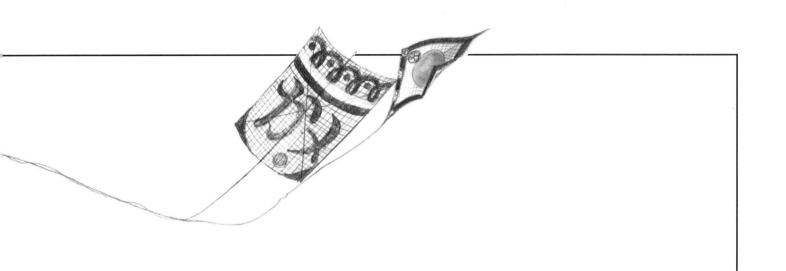

It's really good to be whoever you are—a boy or a girl.

What's important is that both boys
and girls have equal opportunities
for the jobs they want to have,
the way they have fun, and
the life they want to lead.

What do you
want to be when
you grow up?

**Not just one thing!
You could be a . . .**

writer

mother

wife

cook

minister

astronaut

father

husband

cook

*nursery
school
teacher*

secretary

dancer

Make up your own list.

_____

_____

_____

_____

_____

_____

_____

And you may want
to change it when
you get new ideas.

Special Note for Parents and Educators

We need to prepare today's youth for tomorrow's family. In order to communicate mature and responsible attitudes, parents must become the primary sex educators of their own children. We know that silence and evasiveness are just as powerful teachers as are the facts.

Everybody says that parents should be the primary sex educators, but who is preparing the parents for this role? Indeed, in terms of the values and spiritual life of the child, no outside group or agency could replace the family. Thus, we see education for sexuality taking place within the context of the family's value system which, hopefully strives toward a family life free of racism, sexism, and prejudices against people with other values. Most churches and educators officially support this position, but few are doing anything about it.

Studies consistently have revealed that children do not acquire the information they need from parents. It is time for parents to assume this responsibility. Parents, of course, cannot be the sole educators; if they wanted to be, they would have to prevent their children from reading books, newspapers, and magazines; keep them away from television, movies, and public bathrooms; and certainly prohibit them from having any friends at all. Parents are the *main* educators, with schools and religious and community groups as partners in a life-long process.

Society consistently underestimates the capabilities of parents and their children. *You can't tell a child too much: Knowledge doesn't stimulate inappropriate behavior, ignorance does.* If you tell children more than they can understand, they will ask another question or turn you off. Parents must work toward being *askable*. We know most parents want to educate their children, but they are often uncomfortable and don't know how. Obviously, parents who find it difficult to talk to their children about any important issue will not be ready to talk about sex. It seems that most parents are ready, but they want some support.

It is essential for parents to be alert to extremist propaganda and political maneuvering, especially by those groups claiming to have a monopoly on the Judeo-Christian ethic. Censorship in the schools and media is one method used by extremist groups who want to impose their views on everybody. Parents should not be intimidated by scare tactics used as subterfuges for acquiring power on school boards or in churches. In support of these principles, PTA's, foundations, churches, synagogue-related groups, and community organizations can develop ongoing institutes, workshops, seminars, and media presentation. They can put together bibliographies and library and bookstore displays to get the public involved (continuing education is more effective than one-shot lectures). It is expected that religious groups in particular will develop programs based on their own moral beliefs. Community-minded groups should discover opportunities for getting their message heard via public-service options on TV and radio, as well as in newspapers and magazines. We must counter the propaganda that information is harmful or constitutes license for irresponsible behavior. It's time that the "silent" majority expressed itself vigorously, visibly, and vocally.

Selected References

For Younger Children

Did the Sun Shine Before You Were Born—A Sex Education Primer by Sol and Judith Gordon. For children aged 3–7. Developed to help parents communicate facts about sex, reproduction, and the family to their children. Ed-U Press, Fayetteville, N.Y.

Better Safe Than Sorry by Sol and Judith Gordon. A sexual assault prevention book for children aged 3–9, with parents' guide. Ed-U Press, Fayetteville, N.Y.

Bellybuttons Are Navels by Mark Schoen, Ph.D., illustrated by M. J. Quay. Beautifully illustrated story that provides a basic vocabulary for introducing the topics of sexual anatomy and sexual abuse awareness. Prometheus Books, Buffalo, N.Y.

For Teenagers

The Teenage Survival Book by Sol Gordon. A 150-page award-winning publication still considered the most dynamic self-improvement book for youth. Designed to increase self-acceptance. Times Books, New York.

Facts About Sex for Today's Youth by Sol Gordon. Beautifully designed paperback with a traditional approach. Ed-U Press, Fayetteville, N.Y.

Smart Moves: How to Succeed in School, Sports, Career and Life by Dick DeVenzio. Motivates young adults to view their lives and actions in a new and positive way. Prometheus Books, Buffalo, N.Y.

For Parents and Professionals

Raising a Child Conservatively in a Sexually Permissive World by Sol and Judith Gordon. A sensitive, provocative book that's on the cutting edge of parent-child relationships and communication about sexuality in the family. Stresses the role of self-esteem in healthy personality development and approaches the notion of "conservative" from a rational perspective. Fireside, New York.

Experts Advise Parents: A Guide to Raising Loving, Responsible Children, edited by Eileen Shiff. Delacorte, New York.

An End to Shame: Shaping Our Next Sexual Revolution, by Ira L. Reiss, Ph.D., with Harriet M. Reiss. A direct and challenging analysis of America's sexual problems that deals with such important issues as sex education for children, teenage sex, rape, AIDS, pornography, and sex therapy. Prometheus Books, Buffalo, New York.

Photo by Bernard G. Ryle

Dr. Sol Gordon is a clinical psychologist whose areas of special interest include children with learning disabilities and sexuality education. Dr. Gordon received his B.A. and M.S. from the University of Illinois and a Ph.D. in psychology from the University of London.

In his active career of teaching and working in the field of child psychology, he has served as Chief Psychologist of both the Philadelphia Child Guidance Clinic and the Middlesex County Mental Health Clinic in New Brunswick, New Jersey. He has been Associate Professor of Psychology and Director of Project Beacon at Yeshiva University in New York City. He is Professor emeritus of Child and Family Studies at Syracuse University's College for Human Development.

Dr. Gordon's special interest in sexuality education is reflected in the publication of the extremely well-received *Facts About Sex,* hailed as "the best simple book on the subject since 1969" (*Wilson Library Bulletin*), "bone-simple and crystal-clear" (*Voice of Youth Advocates*), and "generally does an excellent job of scotching misinformation and giving the adolescent a good grounding in fact" (*Parents Magazine).*